Francis Frith's

Leicestershire

Photographic Memories

Francis Frith's
Leicestershire

Michael Kilburn

FRITH BOOK Co

First published in the United Kingdom in 1998
by WBC Ltd

Revised paperback edition published in the United Kingdom in 2000
by Frith Book Company Ltd

Paperback Edition 2000
ISBN 1-85937-185-x

Hardback Edition 2002
ISBN 1-85937-580-4

British Library Cataloguing in Publication Data

Francis Frith's Leicestershire
Michael Kilburn

Frith Book Company Ltd
Frith's Barn, Teffont,
Salisbury, Wiltshire SP3 5QP
Tel: +44 (0) 1722 716 376
Email: info@francisfrith.co.uk
www.francisfrith.co.uk

Printed and bound in Great Britain

Front Cover: Leicester, The Clock Tower 1949 L144012

As with any historical database the Frith archive is constantly being corrected and improved and the publishers would welcome information on omissions or inaccuracies

Contents

Francis Frith: *Victorian Pioneer*

Francis Frith, Victorian founder of the world-famous photographic archive, was a complex and multitudinous man. A devout Quaker and a highly successful Victorian businessman, he was both philosophic by nature and pioneering in outlook.

By 1855 Francis Frith had already established a wholesale grocery business in Liverpool, and sold it for the astonishing sum of £200,000, which is the equivalent today of over £15,000,000. Now a multi-millionaire, he was able to indulge his passion for travel. As a child he had pored over travel books written by early explorers, and his fancy and imagination had been stirred by family holidays to the sublime mountain regions of Wales and Scotland. 'What a land of spirit-stirring and enriching scenes and places!' he had written. He was to return to these scenes of grandeur in later years to 'recapture the thousands of vivid and tender memories', but with a different purpose. Now in his thirties, and captivated by the new science of photography, Frith set out on a series of pioneering journeys to the Nile regions that occupied him from 1856 until 1860.

Intrigue and Adventure

He took with him on his travels a specially-designed wicker carriage that acted as both dark-room and sleeping chamber. These far-flung journeys were packed with intrigue and adventure. In his life story, written when he was sixty-three, Frith tells of being held captive by bandits, and of fighting 'an awful midnight battle to the very point of surrender with a deadly pack of hungry, wild dogs'. Sporting flowing Arab costume, Frith arrived at Akaba by camel seventy years before Lawrence, where he encountered 'desert princes and rival sheikhs, blazing with jewel-hilted swords'.

During these extraordinary adventures he was assiduously exploring the desert regions bordering the Nile and patiently recording the antiquities and peoples with his camera. He was the first photographer to venture beyond the sixth cataract. Africa was still the mysterious 'Dark Continent', and Stanley and Livingstone's historic meeting was a decade into the future. The conditions for picture taking confound belief. He laboured for hours in his wicker dark-room in the sweltering heat of the desert, while the volatile chemicals fizzed dangerously in their trays. Often he was forced to work in remote tombs and caves where conditions were cooler. Back in London he exhibited his photographs and was 'rapturously cheered' by members of the Royal Society. His reputation as a photographer was made overnight. An eminent modern historian has likened their impact on the population of the time to that on our own generation of the first photographs taken on the surface of the moon.

Venture of a Life-Time

Characteristically, Frith quickly spotted the opportunity to create a new business as a specialist publisher of photographs. He lived in an era of immense and sometimes violent change. For the poor in the early part of Victoria's reign work was a drudge and the hours long, and people had precious little free time to enjoy themselves. Most had no transport other than a cart or gig at their disposal, and had not travelled far beyond the boundaries of their own town or village. However, by the 1870s, the railways had threaded their way across the country, and Bank Holidays and half-day Saturdays had been made obligatory by Act of Parliament. All of a sudden the ordinary working man and his family were able to enjoy days out and see a little more of the world.

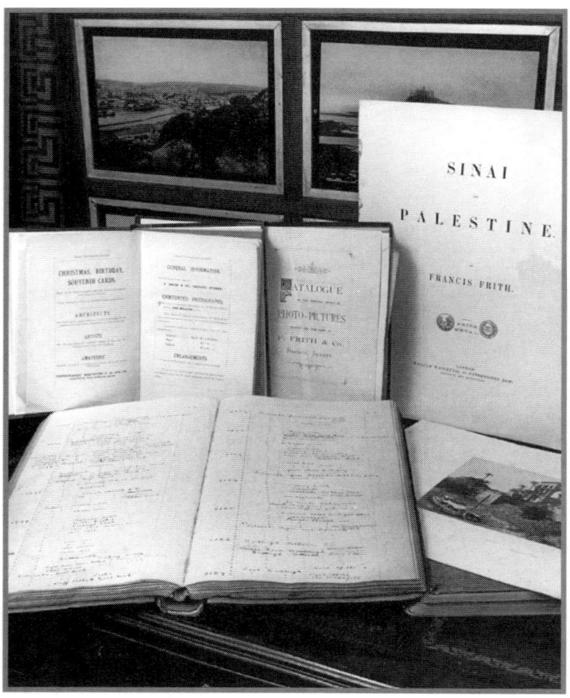

With characteristic business acumen, Francis Frith foresaw that these new tourists would enjoy having souvenirs to commemorate their days out. In 1860 he married Mary Ann Rosling and set out with the intention of photographing every city, town and village in Britain. For the next thirty years he travelled the country by train and by pony and trap, producing fine photographs of seaside resorts and beauty spots that were keenly bought by millions of Victorians. These prints were painstakingly pasted into family albums and pored over during the dark nights of winter, rekindling precious memories of summer excursions.

The Rise of Frith & Co

Frith's studio was soon supplying retail shops all over the country. To meet the demand he gathered about him a small team of photographers, and published the work of independent artist-photographers of the calibre of Roger Fenton and Francis Bedford. In order to gain some understanding of the scale of Frith's business one only has to look at the catalogue issued by Frith & Co in 1886: it runs to some 670 pages, listing not only many thousands of views of the British Isles but also many photographs of most European countries, and China, Japan, the USA and

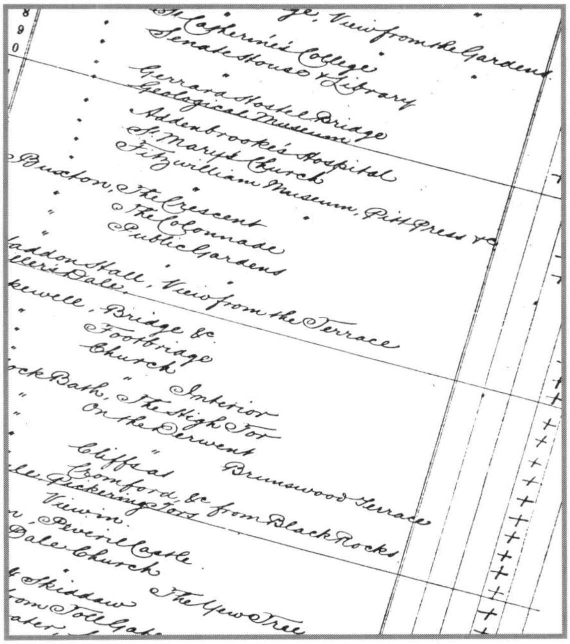
St Catherine's College
Senate House & Library
Gerrard Hostel Bridge
Geological Museum
Addenbrooke's Hospital
St Mary's Church
Fitzwilliam Museum, Pitt Press &c
Buxton, The Crescent
The Colonnade
Public Gardens
Haddon Hall, View from the Terrace
Bridge &c.
Footbridge
Church
Interior
The High Tor
On the Derwent
Cliffs
Brunswood Terrace
Bamford, &c from Black Rocks
Peveril Castle
Dale Church
Skiddaw
The Yew Tree

Canada – note the sample page shown above from the hand-written *Frith & Co* ledgers detailing pictures taken. By 1890 Frith had created the greatest specialist photographic publishing company in the world, with over 2,000 outlets – more than the combined number that Boots and WH Smith have today! The picture on the right shows the *Frith & Co* display board at Ingleton in the Yorkshire Dales. Beautifully constructed with mahogany frame and gilt inserts, it could display up to a dozen local scenes.

Postcard Bonanza

The ever-popular holiday postcard we know today took many years to develop. In 1870 the Post Office issued the first plain cards, with a pre-printed stamp on one face. In 1894 they allowed other publishers' cards to be sent through the mail with an attached adhesive halfpenny stamp. Demand grew rapidly, and in 1895 a new size of postcard was permitted called the court card, but there was little room for illustration. In 1899, a year after Frith's death, a new card measuring 5.5 x 3.5 inches became the standard format, but it was not until 1902 that the divided back came into being, with address and message on one face and a full-size illustration on the other. *Frith & Co* were in the vanguard of postcard development, and Frith's sons Eustace and Cyril continued their father's monumental task, expanding the number of views offered to the public and recording more and more places in Britain, as the coasts and countryside were opened up to mass travel.

Francis Frith died in 1898 at his villa in Cannes, his great project still growing. The archive he created continued in business for another seventy years. By 1970 it contained over a third of a million pictures of 7,000 cities, towns and villages. The massive photographic record Frith has left to us stands as a living monument to a special and very remarkable man.

Frith's Archive: *A Unique Legacy*

Francis Frith's legacy to us today is of immense significance and value, for the magnificent archive of evocative photographs he created provides a unique record of change in 7,000 cities, towns and villages throughout Britain over a century and more. Frith and his fellow studio photographers revisited locations many times down the years to update their views, compiling for us an enthralling and colourful pageant of British life and character.

We tend to think of Frith's sepia views of Britain as nostalgic, for most of us use them to conjure up memories of places in our own lives with which we have family associations. It often makes us forget that to Francis Frith they were records of daily life as it was actually being lived in the cities, towns and villages of his day. The Victorian age was one of great and often bewildering change for ordinary people, and though the pictures evoke an impression of slower times, life was as busy and hectic as it is today.

We are fortunate that Frith was a photographer of the people, dedicated to recording the minutiae of everyday life. For it is this sheer wealth of visual data, the painstaking chronicle of changes in dress, transport, street layouts, buildings, housing, engineering and landscape that captivates us so much today. His remarkable images offer us a powerful link with the past and with the lives of our ancestors.

See Frith at www.francisfrith.co.uk

Today's Technology

Computers have now made it possible for Frith's many thousands of images to be accessed almost instantly. In the Frith archive today, each photograph is carefully 'digitised' then stored on a CD Rom. Frith archivists can locate a single photograph amongst thousands within seconds. Views can be catalogued and sorted under a variety of categories of place and content to the immediate benefit of researchers.

Inexpensive reference prints can be created for them at the touch of a mouse button, and a wide range of books and other printed materials assembled and published for a wider, more general readership - in the next twelve months over a hundred Frith local history titles will be published! The day-to-day workings of the archive are very different from how they were in Francis Frith's time: imagine the herculean task of sorting through eleven tons of glass negatives as Frith had to do to locate a particular sequence of pictures! Yet the archive still prides itself on maintaining the same high standards of excellence laid down by Francis Frith, including the painstaking cataloguing and indexing of every view.

It is curious to reflect on how the internet now allows researchers in America and elsewhere greater instant access to the archive than Frith himself ever enjoyed. Many thousands of individual views can be called up on screen within seconds on one of the Frith internet sites, enabling people living continents away to revisit the streets of their ancestral home town, or view places in Britain where they have enjoyed holidays. Many overseas researchers welcome the chance to view special theme selections, such as transport, sports, costume and ancient monuments.

We are certain that Francis Frith would have heartily approved of these modern developments in imaging techniques, for he himself was always working at the very limits of Victorian photographic technology.

The Value of the Archive Today

Because of the benefits brought by the computer, Frith's images are increasingly studied by social historians, by researchers into genealogy and ancestory, by architects, town planners, and by teachers and schoolchildren involved in local history projects.

In addition, the Frith archive offers every one of us a unique opportunity to examine the places where we and our families have lived and worked down the years. Immensely successful in Frith's own era, the archive is now, a century and more on, entering a new phase of popularity.

The Past in Tune with the Future

Historians consider the Francis Frith Collection to be of prime national importance. It is the only archive of its kind remaining in private ownership and has been valued at a million pounds. However, this figure is now rapidly increasing as digital technology enables more and more people around the world to enjoy its benefits.

Francis Frith's archive is now housed in an historic timber barn in the beautiful village of Teffont in Wiltshire. Its founder would not recognize the archive office as it is today. In place of the many thousands of dusty boxes containing glass plate negatives and an all-pervading odour of photographic chemicals, there are now ranks of computer screens. He would be amazed to watch his images travelling round the world at unimaginable speeds through network and internet lines.

The archive's future is both bright and exciting. Francis Frith, with his unshakeable belief in making photographs available to the greatest number of people, would undoubtedly approve of what is being done today with his lifetime's work. His photographs, depicting our shared past, are now bringing pleasure and enlightenment to millions around the world a century and more after his death.

Leicestershire

The photographs in this volume are historic documents. They record the interregnum between late Victorian development in Leicestershire and the post-1950s boom in housing and office building, which combined with accelerated building technology to deliver the ubiquitous double-glazed window, and almost everything plastic. Notwithstanding the designation of Conservation Areas by sensitive county authorities, which are, by definition, designed to protect the environment, attractive regular terraces and houses have become a hotchpotch of ill-matched windows and doors, through the weaknesses of conservation legislation in its basic form.

To many outsiders, Leicestershire is either to be slept through on the train into or out of St Pancras, or driven through at high speed on the M1 motorway. It is, in fact, an area worthy of special notice, a multi-faceted county of heavy Triassic claylands in the east, and rocky granite and slate outcrops in the west. To insiders, The Shires are evocative words, conjuring up an image of rolling grasslands and sheep, with nucleated villages evenly spaced across the Ordnance Survey map, often linked by straight hawthorn-lined enclosure roads, green drove roads or more ancient ways, quickly proving the old adage that in the countryside you are rarely out of sight of a church spire. Under the grassland, history is preserved in the familiar 'medieval' ridge-and-furrow patterns of selions and furlongs. It is interesting that the patterns are generally referred to as medieval: although recent archaeological evidence points, in some places, to a pre-Conquest date, the remains as we see them must have been in use immediately before the late 18th- or early 19th-century enclosures. I came to this landscape as a child just after the war, when a Sunday outing meant picnicking amongst the hills and hollows of the deserted medieval village of Ingarsby, some four miles east of the city, but it was not until much later, as a schoolboy in 1950, that I came upon W G Hoskins' wonderful little book 'The Heritage of Leicestershire'. Barrows and tumuli, deserted medieval villages, churches and monastic houses were all here, jumping out of the page, and it was through this chance find that a lifetime love-affair with the county began.

Leicestershire is not a county of excesses, and the city will never have the same magnetic effect as York, Bath or Durham. Its one great house, Belvoir Castle, is strangely isolated amongst its lesser but equal neighbours such as Quenby, Baggrave, Withcote or Market Bosworth. Churches such as Stoke Golding, Kings Norton, Gaddesby and Bottesford, and Exton, with its tremendous series of monuments, have a beauty quite equal to those of the more lauded Midland counties of Northamptonshire or Warwickshire. The city, thanks to its extraordinary population explosion during the 19th century, has a good collection of contemporary buildings. An enclave of 18th-century houses survives mainly around St Martins Cathedral, but since the early 1960s little has taken place which could be called enhancement. The Central Ring Road has swept through in accordance with the traffic engineers' cavalier schemes, leaving the historic Newarke Gateway ridiculously isolated and demolishing extensive areas of housing. The city centre has lost some of its visual allure with demolitions to accommodate the Shires shopping centre, but to step out of Trubshaw's Grand Midland Railway Station to be greeted with the well-aired phrase 'eh up me duck', is to be home.

Market Harborough, Leicester Road 72271

Leicester, Belgrave Gate c1949 L144013

In a road of rather mundane buildings is the Palace Theatre, a remarkable building designed in a Moorish style by the Robert Adam of theatre design, Frank Matcham, for Moss Empires in 1901, with a seating capacity of 2,750. After some difficult years the theatre was demolished in 1959. The fine spire of St Marks Church of 1870 makes a worthwhile visual stop to this view north.

Leicester

Roman Leicester occupied some hundred acres to the west of the Clock Tower, and developed around its forum in a standard pattern of gridded streets. After about AD 400, the area became part of the Kingdom of Mercia, and subsequently a part of the Danelaw - this is shown by the 'by' and 'ton' endings to many surrounding village names. Leicester Castle was built soon after the Norman Conquest, and by the 14th century the present open market was established, along with markets for grain, cattle, sheep and fish, among others. Comparatively little survives of the 17th- and 18th-century fabric of the town, but during the 19th-century explosion in the hosiery and boot and shoe industries, the population grew fourteen-fold to over 200,000. This expansion continued into the 20th century, when a number of villages such as Aylestone, Braunstone and Humberstone were absorbed in semi-detached 1930s ribbon development. A Garden City experiment at Humberstone, conceived with Bedford Park and Hampstead Garden Suburb in west and north London in mind, came to little, with only 95 houses built by 1915. At the turn of the 21st century, housing estates of little virtue (Hamilton, for instance) continue to eat away fields and hedgerows until the next outer layer of villages is swallowed.

PHILLIPS
WHY PAY CASH?
EASY TERMS
TURE
BUSES
NARBOROUGH Rd
21

Leicester, Eastgates 1949 L144002

To the young in Leicester in 1949, the Clock Tower seemed like the universe, and life revolved around it guided by policemen on point duty. Holidays were generally taken at Skegness, Mablethorpe or Great Yarmouth; pre-television entertainment was fairly extravagant, with seven cinemas in the town centre, including the Floral Hall, along with three live theatres. Within two miles of the Clock Tower, local cinemas abounded, only to be swept away in the 1960s purge, including the rather magnificent Trocadero at Humberstone, replaced by a petrol station.

Leicester, The Clock Tower 1949 L144012
The Gothic Clock Tower, designed by local architect Joseph Goddard in 1868, is decorated with pinnacles and canopies, along with four Leicester worthies including Alderman Gabriel Newton and Simon de Montfort. Beyond Corts Limited can be seen the dominant dome of the Opera House, demolished in 1960, where each year the Christmas pantomime was staged, and appreciated with thunderous applause.

Leicester, Market Street 1949 L144016

The Edwardian and Victorian buildings in this part of the City are efficient without being distinctive. Closing the view south is the former General Accident Building of 1932, which Pevsner rather unkindly sums up as 'a vile, impertinent lump'.

Leicester, Belvoir Street c1949 L144017

In the centre is the dome of the Grand Hotel, built in 1898 to the designs of Cecil Ogden, and dismissed by Pevsner as 'of no architectural value', perhaps an over-critical view. In Belvoir Street in 1949, Cowlings Record Shop was much frequented by Leicester's youth, who could sit in booths and hear the records before deciding whether or not to buy.

Leicester, Granby Street 1949 L144032
Banks abound in Granby Street: the Italianate National Westminster of 1869, the Midland, a Gothic creation with its French pavilion roof, and the Yorkshire Penny Bank opposite the Grand Hotel is probably the most striking of all. Also in Granby Street is the sparkling turn-of-the-century Turkish Cafe offering a breath of the orient.

Leicester, Gallowtree Gate c1960 L144104
Thomas Cook started his travel business from a building overlooking the Clock Tower in 1841, and the front commemorating this historic undertaking, put up in 1894, is, indeed, special. The building on the left fronts the open market, said to be the biggest in Europe, with access ways running between the shops.

Leicester, Humberstone Gate 1949 L144007

How well ordered this street scene appears, with virtually no cars, only rumbling trams, and great six-wheeler buses. The Bell Hotel speaks of genteel days, and Lewis's store on the right speaks of a more pressurised era of merchandising in the 1930s. It is sad that a high proportion of the buildings in this photograph have been demolished in recent years.

◄ **Leicester, The Roman Forum and Jewry Wall c1955** L144069

The remains of Ratae Coritanorum, the origins of the city and a regional capital, lie adjacent to the superb Saxon church of St Nicholas, seen here in the centre of the photograph. The forum and basilica were excavated by Kathleen Kenyon. The remains are situated at the top of the High Street and are a must, particularly for the first-time visitor to the City.

Leicester, Price Rupert's Gateway, Castle Yard c1955 L144091

The mid 12th-century Great Hall of Robert le Bossu survives in Castle Yard; up to modern times it has been in use as an Assizes Court and Crown Court. In 1645 the castle was besieged by Prince Rupert and King Charles and captured, only to be retaken by Parliamentarians following the Royalist defeat at Naseby. The gateway has been ruined since 1832. Masked by the gate is the collegiate church of St Mary de Castro, beautiful outside, but with a dull interior.

Leicester, Granby Street 1949 L144035

As Granby Street sweeps right towards the Clock Tower, the photograph clearly illustrates the unspectacular variety of buildings to be seen in the city centre. At the time of this photograph there are no roof extensions, few ugly street signs and no pedestrianisation.

Leicester, The Guildhall, Guildhall Lane c1949 L144025

Leicester grew rapidly in the 18th and 19th centuries, but it continued to be governed from its small medieval Guildhall until 1876. Situated among the somewhat reduced remains of the buildings of Georgian Leicester, now tightly grouped in New Street, Peacock Lane and Friar Lane, the Guildhall is overshadowed by St Martins Cathedral (upgraded in 1927 from parish church status). The spire of the church is of the moment, but it was worked on internally by G E Street and J L Pearson at the end of the 19th century. To the rear of the Guildhall, in 1949, was Alderman Newton's Boys Grammar School, the resited 18th-century foundation of Alderman Gabriel Newton, who now lies buried in the churchyard of All Saints, High Cross Street. A visit to the Guildhall is worthwhile, with its amazing 14th-century timbered Great Hall of the Corpus Christi Guild, and the intimate inner courtyard of All Saints, High Cross Street is also worth seeing.

Leicester, De Montfort Hall, University Road c1955 L144118

A surprisingly spry 85-year-old building, the De Montfort Hall shows little sign of ageing. Designed by architect Shirley Harrison, the building is well-sited close to Victoria Park, and to Lutyens' War Memorial, dedicated to those who fell in the First World War. To the rear of the Hall is the university campus, with buildings by Denys Lasdun and James Stirling.

◄ **Leicester, The Town Hall, Horsefair Street c1955** L144074

Thirty years prior to the building of the new Town Hall, Leicester was in a dreadful sanitary condition, with privies literally overflowing into the streets, and it was not until the mid 1850s that piped water came to the town, along with the first sewers. By the 1870s facilities were expanding, and with this expansion came a new bureaucracy.

Leicester Tudor Arch c1955 ► L144093

◄ **Leicester, Interior of the De Montfort Hall c1955** L144125

With clear visibility and excellent acoustics, De Montfort Hall is one of the Midlands' finest concert venues. Over the years it has heard every kind of music, and played host to many school speech days.

Boots
CHEMISTS
Boots
Boots
Coppock LTD
MARTINS
DYERS & CLEANERS
COATS
HILTONS
BOOTS
HILTONS
SHOES
LEICESTER EVENING
MAIL

Loughborough

The medieval street pattern, the parish church of All Saints and a ruined 15th-century hall house, which emerged in 1962 during the demolition of the rectory, serves as the very scant evidence of old Loughborough.
Second in size to Leicester itself, this rather dull, red-brick town was established with an open market by 1220; the November Fair followed a decade or so later. As it was situated eleven miles from Leicester, and on the Leicester/Derby road, turnpiked in 1726, the town's coaching trade was assured. In 1794 the River Soar was canalised, and with this new accessibility to the waterway network, the hosiery and engineering industries began to settle locally. To ensure the town's long-term future in commerce, the railway arrived in 1840, not only to transport the town's products, but also to carry coal from nearby pits. In more recent years the town has bathed in the glory of its university.

Loughborough, High Street 1955 L197003
A policeman on point duty sets the tone of this well-regulated scene. Above Harris's shop is a glimpse of industrially prosperous Loughbrough, with Brush Electrical and J Taylor's bell foundry in Cobden Street being among the more widely known resident companies.

▼ Loughborough, The Market Place 1954 L197050

This is a model medieval market place in its wide, long configuration. There is little remarkable about the buildings, which are mainly of the 19th century. All Saints Church, seen in the background, grew in tandem with the town's increasing prosperity, and justifies a close inspection.

▼ Loughborough, Market Place c1965 L197101

Since 1955 two architectural nonentities have appeared on the right of the photograph to mar the already indifferent quality of the market place, and road markings are becoming a prominent feature. The Italianate Town Hall dominates the street scene with its rather odd bell-cote.

▲ Loughborough, The Market Place c1955
L197009

Lloyds bank, on the left, provides a datum from which the quality of Loughborough's architecture can be measured. Apart from a few earlier buildings in the shot, all is rather mediocre. Restrained signs and shop fronts and no unsightly yellow lines speak of an almost forgotten era.

◄ **Loughborough, High Street c1955** L197008
The High Street (the A6 Leicester/Derby road) becomes Leicester Road as it runs south. A few earlier buildings survive on the left-hand side of the photograph, but the right is dominated by uninspired, even dreary, red-brick Edwardian buildings.

LADIES &
GENTLEMENS
HAIRDRESSING

Loughborough, Church Gate c1955
L197001

◄ **Loughborough, College Gate, Ashby Road c1955** L197026
Hazlerigg Hall and Rutland Hall, built to the designs of the then County Education Committee Architect in 1939 in a neo-Tudor style, were the original halls of residence to Loughborough College. Expanded after 1952, the now University of Technology occupies a campus approaching 250 acres.

◄ **Loughborough, Devonshire Square c1955** L197021

Although the Gothic hotel has some claim to architectural quality, it is the Art Deco intruder which catches the eye. Faced in cream tiles and built in 1936, the cinema must have proved irresistible to its original audiences seeking escape into fantasy, as did their predecessors in the elaborate world of Victorian theatre.

▼ **Loughborough, Queens Park, Granby Street c1960** L197045

The view from the typically landscaped municipal park is enlivened by the attractive Central Library building of 1903, with its Baroque facade and conical roof crowned by a timber belt turret. Behind the library are examples of the town's modest turn-of the-century housing stock.

◄ **Loughborough, The Carillon, Queens Park c1955** L197017

This 150ft high, 47-bell brick carillon was designed by Sir Walter Tapper, and erected in 1923 as the town's tribute to the fallen of the First World War. The bells were cast by Taylors, whose foundry was established in Loughborough in 1839 and with Whitechapel, London, comprises England's only surviving bell founders.

Barrow-upon-Soar, High Street c1965 B514029
The rather barren appearance of the High Street exemplified in this photograph sets the tenor of this large mainly red-brick village. It is difficult not to greet the intrusive 'modern' post office to the right of the photograph with a certain sadness.

◄ **Barrow-upon-Soar, Holy Trinity Church c1965**
B514006
Externally, the Mountsorrel granite facing of the church gives it a hard, almost unwelcoming appearance. Most of the building work was carried out between 1863 and 1870, to the designs of Stevens and Robinson, a Derbyshire firm of architects. Internally, there is a mid 17th-century monument to Theophilus Cave, and one from the mid 18th century to Martha Utber.

Barrow-upon-Soar & Quorn

The village of Barrow-upon-Soar is situated about eight miles north of Leicester, with the river and the limeworks its main claims to any fame. Since at least the medieval period, the lime produced at Barrow has, for building purposes, been the best. Few buildings in the village are worthy of note, apart from the Old Men's Hospital founded by Humphrey Babington in 1686 and the Old Women's Hospital of 1825. One 17th-century house of any note survives in Beveridge Street.

The mention of Quorn immediately brings to mind one of the premier English hunts, probably only to be equalled in fame by the Belvoir; it is a pity that the village fails to reflect the colourful splendour associated with its namesake. Its medieval church of Norman foundation houses good monuments, in particular one of 1587 to Sir John Farnham, by Epiphanius Evesham, whose fine cutting and virtuosity in design raises him above almost every other English sculptor of the 16th century. Many of the village houses are built of local granite and Swithland slate, and Bridge Mills pays tribute to the village as a place of manufacturing.

◄ **Barrow-upon-Soar, The Bridge and the River c1965** B514032
By 1086 the Soar Valley was well settled, and although the Domesday village of Barhou offers little to delight the visitor, the river has a watery magnetism which draws families from Leicester to its banks on warm summer days.

▼ **Barrow-upon-Soar, The Boathouse c1965** B5143271
The charm of the river is highlighted in this classic composition of moored boats, overhanging trees, and a perfectly-positioned swan - the ultimate vision of a lazy day spent away from traffic and stress.

▼ **Quorn, The Hurst Hotel c1965** Q11020
This is a classic Edwardian hotel, with its tile-hung gables, bracketed enclosed balcony and original fenestration. On the right, a contemporary wing of singular quality lurks behind the petrol pumps. For show, transportation of an earlier age adorns the forecourt.

▲ **Quorn, High Street c1965** Q11018
The village sits astride the A6, only two miles north of Mountsorrel, and although deeply embedded in granite country, the buildings in the photograph lack any of that hard-edged quality. Red-brick workers' cottages face timber and render on the opposite side of the road, speaking of softer parts of the country.

Quorn, The River Soar c1965 Q11004
A swan cruises on the river as it curves into the east side of the village, running by a municipalised garden of finely-mown grass, and a statutory wooden seat carefully placed under the only tree of consequence.

◄ **Mountsorrel, The Green c1960** M2363269
Hardly picturesque, crouched under the outcrop of granite, is a collection of small cottages, the earlier one probably occupied by the granite workers who came from as far away as Scotland to quarry and work the hard stone.

Mountsorrel

It is said that Mountsorrel had more pubs for its size than anywhere else in the country, presumably to cater for the influx of quarry workers. Since the 18th century the town has been the birthplace of numberless pink granite setts and kerb-stones; these were originally for the turnpike, but some spread by waterway, countrywide. Working the hard stone produced great amounts of waste; this eventually took over quarry production, and granite chippings, particularly useful for railway ballast, were made.

Granted market status in 1292, the town was more famous for its fair. The domed rotunda stands in the market place and was built in 1793, but even this addition does little to enliven the area. It is difficult to enthuse about either of the town's two churches, St Peter's, basically medieval and built in local granite, and Christ Church, built around 1845 and of little interest. This is a town for the industrial archaeologist, where granite and slate blend together by the former wharves of the canal.

◄ **Mountsorrel, Market Place c1960** M2363270
Remnants of the Earl of Leicester's castle which was destroyed in the early 13th century can still be seen in this rather dismal but interesting village. The plain red brick house is, however, a veritable gem, built around 1780 and prominent towards the left of the photograph.

◄ **Mountsorrel, The River Soar c1960**
M2363268
To the east of the village, the canalised river was heavily used for carrying stone, and waggon tipplers for loading up the boats can still be seen. The pleasure craft in the photograph emphasise the failure of the canals for industrial transportation.

Woodhouse Eaves

Woodhouse Eaves, situated in the heart of the ancient forest of Charnwood, first appears as Wodehuses, literally meaning the houses in the woods, around 1210. With its close neighbour, Swithland, it is associated with a vast output of slate during the 18th and 19th centuries, which was used as a roofing material and for graveyard headstones. Its ability to take the most intricate of carving and to weather well put it among the most popular of materials, to such an extent that almost every churchyard in the county can show examples - which are often used as paving these days. During the 19th century an influx of Welsh slate overwhelmed the local quarries. In Swithland Wood, to the south of the village, the disused slate workings can be seen amongst the bluebells, for which the area was well known. Overlooking the village, Windmill Hill was crowned by one of the county's post mills until it was destroyed by fire in 1945.

Woodhouse Eaves, From the Memorial c1955
W367041
In walking country, the village, although undistinguished, is associated by local people with Newton Linford, Bradgate Park and Beacon Hill, or just as being on the back route from Leicester to Shepshed. The garage on the extreme right of the photograph emphasises the easy pace of 1950s motoring.

◄ **Woodhouse Eaves**
The Village c1955

W367010

St Pauls Church of 1837, by William Railton, dominates the village with its intricate pattern of roofs. Railton exhibited at the Royal Academy, and was architect to the Church Commissioners from 1838-48. Apart from working in Leicestershire, he designed Nelson's Column in Trafalgar Square and was also employed on Ripon Minster, Yorkshire.

◄ **Woodhouse Eaves, Main Street c1955** W367053
Quarrymen's cottages, and the archetypal Pear Tree pub, give no hint of the attractions of the surrounding countryside. Bradgate Park, only a stone's throw away, where Lady Jane Grey, the ill-fated nine-day queen, lived in the now ruined house, is a favourite beauty spot away from the city.

Woodhouse Eaves, View from Old John c1960 ► W367089
Crowning the highest point in Bradgate Park, the views from this 18th-century prospect tower are among the finest in the county. Although given to and administered by the City Council since 1928, the much-visited park, enclosed in c1250, has not lost any of its essential rugged character.

◄ **Woodhouse Eaves, Charnwood Forest Convalescent Home c1955** W367024
After the war, to be ill as a child was considered worthwhile if it meant spending time away by being sent to the home to recuperate. It was, however, always just as good to return home again.

◄ **Rothley, St Mary and St John the Baptist Church c1955** R259010
The large size of this Charnwood commuter village is hardly reflected in such an idyllic scene as this, a curving roadway with modest houses leading directly to the west door of the 13th-century church, housing a good series of monuments. In the churchyard is a cross shaft dating, it is said, to the 9th century.

Rothley

Rothley lies some five miles to the north of Leicester, and to the west of the busy A6. Although the village is close to the River Soar, it was not until the arrival of the railway that it began to expand. An early housing estate was laid out around 1910 by Parker and Unwin, who were much involved in the design of the famous pioneering development of Hampstead Garden Suburb, London. Thomas Babington Macaulay, Rothley's most famous son, was born at Rothley Temple on St Crispin's Day, 1800, the son of the anti-slaver, Zachary Macaulay. Thomas became the Whig MP for Calne, Leeds, but it was his masterpiece - 'A History of England', that brought him undying fame. In historic building terms, the Temple is one of the most important houses in the county, and as Rothley Court Hotel, it is readily accessible. The village is rich in vernacular houses, and the visitor will not be unrewarded.

◄ **Rothley, Woodgate 1951** R259002
Here we see the mundane suburban face of the village, which has grown around a core of rather special later medieval houses and the Rothley Temple, built on Knights Templar land in c1315. Along with Temple Church, London and Temple Balsall, Warwickshire, the chapel is one of the finest in England.

◄ **Rothley, Milking Time c1955** R259001
A scene which is familiar to us all, even in the rush of today's 'rat-run' world. Plodding cows head for the milking parlour, guided by the farmer on his wobbly upright bicycle.

▲ **Belvoir Castle, From the Air c1960** B633078

Belvoir Castle is picturesquely situated some six miles to the west of Grantham, at the foot of a narrow spur jutting up between Nottinghamshire and Lincolnshire. Prominent for miles around, it was built menacingly by the Conqueror's standard bearer, Robert de Todeni, on an escarpment rising some two hundred feet above the surrounding countryside.

◄ **Belvoir Castle, From the north-west 1890** 27861

This classic view of the castle contrasts the delicacy of the chapel, with its triple Gothic windows and pinnacled octagonal towers, with the somewhat more robust Windsor-like tower to its left.

Belvoir Castle & Bottesford

Deriving from 'beautiful view', the name equates with the French Belvedre, and is first recorded in 1130 as Beleder. By the mid 15th century the original castle was ruinous, but it was rebuilt during the second quarter of the 16th century. Ruinous again by 1649, it was rebuilt at the wish of the Countess of Rutland by the pupil of Inigo Jones, Philip Webb. In 1801, the prolific yet masterly architect, James Wyatt, was engaged to remodel the building. The task was in fact completed by the Reverend Sir John Thoroton after fire partially destroyed the new work, Wyatt having died.

In 1076, to the north of the castle, Robert de Todeni endowed a small Benedictine priory with only four monks, so that he and his wife could be buried. It was dissolved in 1538 and demolished. The bodies of the founder and his wife were recovered and reinterred in the present chapel.

Faced in yellow ironstone, this fairytale composition is the ideal castle of 19th-century romantic fiction, with its towers and crenellations breathing life into the Gothic fantasy world. The aerial photograph shows an apparently unstructured plan, but the castle is in fact roughly rectangular around a central courtyard. On the right-hand side of the building is the Regents Gallery, transformed by Wyatt from the earlier long gallery, and to the left is the Elizabeth Saloon, named after the fifth Duchess of Rutland. Outside the thick wooded cover, the more open land of the deer park is corrugated by the medieval ridge and furrow of open cultivation.

The most northerly village in Leicestershire, this large parish sits comfortably on the River Devon. An expansive village, its buildings of interest tend to be distributed rather than grouped. The Rectory in Church Street is now without interest, while Flemings Almshouses and the Earl of Rutland's Hospital should be noted. Flemings Bridge of the 17th century lies close by St Mary's Church.

▲

Bottesford, St Mary's Church c1960 B515003

The recessed crocketted spire of St Mary's dominates the countryside around. Inside, the church houses one of the finest collections of monuments in the country. Superb works of art commissioned since 1543 to mark the resting places of the Earls of Rutland include two of considerable elegance by Grinling Gibbons.

& Co GENERAL DRAPERS
HOVIS
CROCKATTS

Melton Mowbray

Melton Mowbray, a Domesday village, some fifteen miles north-east of Leicester, takes the second part of its name from the Norman lord Roger de Mowbray, who lived here in about 1125. This quite small town has three remarkable claims to fame. Firstly, it can safely be called the fox-hunting capital of the Shires; here, up to the Second World War, royalty could come unmolested to ride during the day and flirt during the night. Secondly, the town is the home of the world-famous pork pie, which was probably invented to feed hungry huntsmen as early as the 14th century. The recipe has changed over the years: the original contained currants, raisins and anchovies, as well as pork. The town's third claim to fame is its association with Stilton cheese, which originated at Quenby Hall, to the south of the town, and was first called Quenby Cheese. The real cheese is made at Melton and its surrounding villages. Park the car, visit the church and purchase two gastronomic delights before moving on.

Melton Mowbray
Sherrard Street c1955 M60072

Although the bicycle is making a comeback in the 1990s, the sight of so many propped against the kerb and quite happily left is past. A large chain and stout lock are today's essentials - or, better still, remove the front wheel before leaving.

◄ **Melton Mowbray, Nottingham Street c1955** M60031

The early 19th-century Bell Hotel dominates this lively street scene, with its vital interaction of stalls, traffic and people, now so often lost in the bromide world of pedestrianisation. Further along the street the former Italianate Corn Exchange with its rather odd timber bell tower can be seen.

◄ **Melton Mowbray, South Parade c1960**

M60097

In this predominately 19th-century street, it is the once-familiar that takes the eye: the delivery boy with his white coat and bicycle basket, and the unattended pram outside Mason's shop - in today's world this is no longer even a possibility for the modern mother.

▼ **Melton Mowbray, The Town Centre c1960** M60094

Older buildings are to be found behind the innocuous facades of 18th- and 19th-century prosperity in Melton, which was boosted by its being at the centre of the hunting world, and by its prosperous sheep market.

◄ **Melton Mowbray, Market Place 1932**

85169

Crowds gather under tented canopies and around trestle-tabled market stalls to snatch up bargains, just as they have done for 500 years. Good 18th-century buildings dominate the scene. Note the former Swan Inn of the late 17th century on the extreme right of the photograph.

◄ **Melton Mowbray, St Mary's Church 1927**

80309

This is probably the most beautiful of all Leicestershire churches, floating here above the trees and grassland, its magnificent late 15th-century tower dominating the market place and the south side of the town. The fine porch once provided cover for the town fire engine.

Melton Mowbray, Burton Street c1955
M60079
Burton Street refers to the former leper hospital of St Mary and St Lazarus established about 1150 by Robert de Mowbray, to the south of the town; it can only be seen now as a series of earthworks to the north of Burton Lazarus Hall.

Melton Mowbray, St Mary's Church, North Transept 1927
80313
Paid for by the priory of Lewes in Sussex in about 1300, the architecture represents a triumph of the stone mason's art, so much so that the church was championed as a possible contender for the new cathedral in 1926. The elaborate brass chandelier dates from 1746.

Melton Mowbray, Anne of Cleves' House, Burton Street c1955 M60011
One of the finest houses in the town and dating from the 15th century, this is likely to have been built as a priest's lodging. The name is linked to the church's connection with Lewes Priory and its revenues, which became the Queen's jointure.

MELTON FARMERS
OFFICE

Melton Mowbray, The Cattle Market c1955

M60027

The clothes of the traders may have changed, but Melton has been at the centre of the sheep farming industry for a number of centuries. Sheep farming in this area started from a time in the 15th century when the people of villages such as Ingarsby were ejected, and the more profitable sheep were moved in by the monks of Leicester Abbey.

Melton Mowbray, The Cattle Market c1955 M60028
The sheep, destined to become English mutton, may look bored, but to these men they are living money. Any fluctuation in prices can mean the difference between considerable wealth or months of hard work all for nothing.

Melton Mowbray, Lady Wilton's Bridge, Egerton Park c1960 M60068
The elegant, five-arched ashlar bridge of around 1830 is named after the Countess of Wilton, whose husband - a well-known figure in the hunting world - bought Egerton Lodge and entertained the rich and famous until he died in 1882.

Melton Mowbray, St Egelwin The Martyr, Scalford c1955 M60012
This church lies to the north of Melton Mowbray; built of ironstone and limestone, it dates from the late 12th century, with a south aisle of c1270. The tower was rebuilt around 1640, and the rather solid-looking chancel was added in 1845. There are now notable fitments and fittings in the church.

Melton Mowbray, The Scalford Hunt c1955 M60056
Whether it is something to love or to hate, the hunt with all its colourful trappings has brought much-needed employment to the Shires since the 18th century. Tradition, spectacle and danger are here, bound tightly to the timeless bond between man and horse, and man and dog.

CHURCH LANE
727 LDE

Asfordby

The Leicestershire industrial landscape has never been dramatic, but the ironworks at Asfordby Hill provided a microcosmic taste of the North country. Built by the Stanton and Staveley companies in 1878 on the ironstone belt, the five blast furnaces brought with them an inevitable backwash. Once small and well-sited above the River Wreake, the village absorbed an ultimately visually destructive share of the housing needed to cater for the inevitable influx of workers with their families, until the closure of the complex in 1958.

Asfordby, Church Lane c1960 A211025
Apart from All Saints, little of architectural quality has survived, except for a few rather handsome houses, including the Rectory of 1808 and the Old Hall. This view of the church, and on to the river behind, retains a tranquil air uncommon to much of the village.

◄ **Asfordby, All Saints Church c1960** A211003
The 15th-century spire soars above the River Wreake on its south side, with the now rather mundane Village Street to its north. Internally, there is little to detain the visitor, apart from the nave roof with its stone heads and wooden angels.

▲ **Asfordby, The River Wreake c1960** A211020
Out of the River Eye, to the east of Melton Mowbray, flows the River Wreake, slowly winding its way around the superb earthworks of Kirby Park and the former Augustinian priory at Kirby Bellars to the south of Asfordby village

▼ **Asfordby, The Old Hall, Main Street c1960** A211008
Formerly the manor house of about 1620, this fine red brick building is now itself deteriorating. Sashed windows, within stone surrounds under triple gables, grace a quietly elegant facade. Internally Jacobean woodwork survives, as does a wooden spiral back stair. Facing Main Street is the early 19th-century coach-house and stable to The Old Hall.

Asfordby, Main Street c1960 A211001
The late 19th-century industrial face of the village percolates through the photograph, providing a dramatic contrast to Church Lane, which runs almost picturesquely away to the right of the cross.

Queniborough, The Village Street c1955
Q12003

Queniborough has the good fortune to be sited away from major roads, although it has become almost joined to industrial Syston. The main street is wide, with a fine collection of houses of various dates, styles and materials. In the photograph only the telegraph pole and its wires intrude into the scene.

Queniborough & Syston

Queniborough, The Village and St Mary's Church c1955 Q12001
Although Queniborough is virtually a part of the outer edge of suburban Leicester, this photograph presents an almost chocolate-box view of the village. The thatched cruck cottage, with its museum-piece petrol pump and the amazing interlocking of roofs, lead the eye inexorably to the needle-like spire, which crowns the pink granite tower of the church. Internally, the building lacks any quality monuments, apart from a brass plate commemorating Margaret Bury, who died in 1633. In the early 1980s, vestry and complimentary rooms were built into the west end of the church.

Syston, The Memorial & High Street c1955
S488016
A rather choleric lion sits on top of a strangely classical island memorial cum clock tower. The total street scene exudes 1900, with typical shops and corner pub.

Billesdon

Billesdon is to be seen on foot. It is oblong in plan, with the church at its southern end and the A47 to the north, running from east to west. Long-abandoned medieval roads enter the village: in particular from the north from Cold Newton, itself a shrunken medieval village, and from Gaulby to the south-west, through the deserted medieval village of Frisby, into the narrow back lanes of Billesdon. Although it is not picturesque in a picture-book way, this is a village to absorb at leisure.

Billesdon, Back Street c1955 B593006
Diverse materials make up the warp and weft of this village. At the southern end of Back Street, mud walls survive opposite the 17th-century Old School building, and the turn-of-the-century Stone House displays the builder's artful use of a cheaper brick shell adorned with a more expensive stone front.

Billesdon, The Market Place c1955 B593002

The A47 Leicester-Uppingham road forms one side of the roughly triangular market place; although the photograph shows, in the main, modest cottages of 17th- and 18th-century date, more impressive houses are to be found behind the camera. Until recently the long established Geary Brothers, builders and joiners, occupied the building to the right. The Friday market was discontinued at the end of the 18th century. Not only does the ancient 'Jurassic Trackway' run on a north-south line to the east of the village towards Tilton-on-the Hill, but a Neolithic road from Leicester, eastwards towards Ingarsby, skirts the northern boundary of the parish. In its turn that same road line was utilised to demarcate part of the boundary to the Saxon estate belonging to Tochi, now translated as Tugby, a village three miles to the east of Billesdon. In this north-western sector of a remarkable parish it is possible to go back two thousand years at a glance, from the ancient trackway to an abandoned railway line, courtesy of Dr Beeching. Also within this very small area is Billesdon Coplow, a prominent wooded hill, and within its lee Botany Bay fox covert, which is thus clearly dated soon after 1788, when the infamous penal colony was established in Australia.

Billesdon, From the South-West c1955 B593001
Close to the village, medieval ridge and furrow cultivation has been preserved in its meadows and closes, and on its western edge the back lanes seem to be in an unusually complete state. Many houses have their front doors opening directly onto alleyways and paths, all apparently higgledy-piggledy, saying much about the layout and texture of medieval village life, always under the shadow of the church.

Billesdon, From the East c1955 B593004
This view, taken from the fields beyond the village, shows the broach spire of the church of St John the Baptist, rebuilt in 1861, rising above the very attractive slate and stone roofscape of a village of mainly brick and ironstone-faced houses.

Oakham & Cottesmore

Oakham is the county town of Rutland, a proud name which has recently been rightly restored after the 1970s fiasco, when it was obliterated by merging it into Leicestershire. The town has remained small, notwithstanding some 20th-century expansion particularly on its western fringes; since the creation of Rutland Water, it has become an ideal centre from which to sample its aquatic pleasures. For the walker, excursions to the beautiful Elizabethan church at Brook, or to the great house and church at Burley-on-the-Hill, should not prove arduous. In the town centre there are few disruptive elements: the golden stone of the buildings enhances views along the High Street, and in particular the area around the market place. The surviving hall within the castle earthworks served as a local court room until 1970, with its famous collection of horseshoes occupying much of the wall space, each donated by peers of the realm on their first visits to the town. The interest of Oakham is generally concentrated into a comparatively small area, but visitors should allow time to wander.

Oakham,
The Castle and All Saints Church 1927 80295
This is a beautiful group. The 14th-century tower and spire of the parish church dominates the market place and school to its south, while to the east, the castle remains combine to produce the classic juxtaposition of lordly and ecclesiastical dominance.

Oakham, All Saints Church, Nave and Chancel 1927 80290
The church is an elegant creation of around 1300, with a tall, slim five-bay arcade and clerestorey, creating a tremendous feeling of space. The arcade capitals are carved with biblical scenes, mixed up with birds and animals. The flower-decked font is dated around 1225.

Oakham, The Hawthorn Horse 1932 85153
This horse represents a supremely ironic comment. Here is the hunter, bred to cross in safety the open pastures of the Shires, formed in the enclosures' favourite hedge-planting material, which makes up the obstacles to its safe progress.

Cottesmore c1955 C434011
Cottesmore is a typical limestone and ironstone village, set in a region of rolling, spired landscapes of hedges and walls in country which the hunt can, in the main, take in its stride. Cottesmore is now part of Rutland, a tiny county which seems, apart from blips such as the cement works at Ketton, never to have moved into any industrial age, or even into an age of mass communication.

◄ **Uppingham, High Street c1955** U10013
Uppingham is a particularly charming town with an attractive series of 17th- and 18th-century buildings. Surprisingly, the shop fronts in the photograph, have, in the main, been preserved, presumably at the behest of a vigilant local council. The street bustles today in the best possible way.

Uppingham

As attractive as almost any Midland market town, Uppingham is surrounded by stone villages of outstanding quality. To the south is Lyddington, with its wide main street and Bede House, originally a part of the Bishop of Lincoln's palace, now in the care of English Heritage; a mile or so to its west is Stoke Dry, a single street on a steep hill running down to Eye Brook Reservoir. Here is a church where the Gunpowder Plotters are said to have met and lingered, with its strange carving, wall paintings, and Digby monuments. To the north of the town, and almost in a line from east to west, are the stone villages of Wing, with its mazes, Preston and Ridlington.

When W G Hoskins wrote his 'Shell Guide to Rutland' in 1963, he noted specially that motoring in the county was still a pleasure. To a great extent those days have gone, but even now, once away from the main roads, backwaters such as atmospheric Stockerston, Brooke or Tixover can be enjoyed in peace. The area will provide a relaxing, unhurried weekend. Park the car, walk or cycle and just soak up the landscape.

◄ **Uppingham, The Market Place 1932** 85156
Little seems to have altered in the market place since the 18th century. The square seems quite small now for a town which has had an extremely active market since the 13th century. The grand church of St Peter and St Paul, which oversees the goings-on, is from the 14th century, but it was badly mauled in a restoration of 1842.

◄ **Uppingham, Uppingham School, High Street 1927** 80317
During the medieval period, grammar schools were founded for the education of scholars across the class spectrum, but by the 18th century, the so-called Great Schools had arrived in England. Founded in 1584 by Archdeacon Johnson in a single-roomed building, the Uppingham School complex expanded vastly during the last century.

◀ **Uppingham, The Victoria Tower, High Street 1922** 72280

The tower has provided a daunting welcome to generations of potential pupils. Although appearing to be medieval, it was designed by Sir Thomas Jackson in 1815. In the recess is a statue of the school's founder by Sir George Frampton.

▲ **Uppingham, Uppingham School, High Street 1932** 85164

Whereas Harrow School occupies buildings spread out along the main village streets, Uppingham takes on the qualities of a university, being, in the main, laid out around quadrangles. The buildings range in date from the end of the 16th century to those of Drew-Edwards Keen of the 1980s.

▼ **Uppingham, St Peter and St Paul's Church and the School 1932** 85159

This panoramic view of the church and school from flower-bedecked meadowland sums up the qualities of this self-contained town. In 1932, England was not familiar with today's chemically controlled, monocrop pastures, nor was it a challenge to buy home grown fruit in the shops.

Uppingham, The School Quadrangle 1927 80323
The air of a monastic undercroft, with its heavy circular columns and chamfered pointed arches, pervades the photograph. Architectural greats such as G E Street, Ernest Newton and later Oliver Hill worked on the school buildings, a classic collection of their kind.

Market Harborough, High Street 1922 72262

The High Street, earlier called the Great Street, is lined either side with Georgian buildings which sit at the head of earlier burgage plots, much the same as at Uxbridge, Middlesex or St Ives, Huntingdonshire. The wide street provided the place where townsfolk and country visitors could barter or sell goods on a day-to-day basis, and it widens considerably either side of the church - this is more apparent from the air.

Market Harborough & Great Bowden

The town developed as a deliberately-created market centre at the crossing of the River Welland, growing up within the parish of Great Bowden some time around 1175; it was granted a weekly market in 1202. The superb church with its spire, said to be among the best in England, has no churchyard and no rights to carry out burials; this responsibility is incumbent upon the mother church. In the 18th century, Market Harborough was little more than one great market street, but with the turnpiked road and the arrival of the Grand Union Canal along with the railway, industry began to settle in the town. Factories making carpets and footwear appeared close to the centre, as did warehouses and a corn mill. Now the main roads are built up with turn-of-the-century and later red-brick housing, the cinema on the Northampton Road has closed, and small supermarkets are springing up, just like any other town.

The Lordship of Great Bowden, a royal soke, and Market Harborough has always been as one, although a Domesday population of 49 was recorded at Great Bowden; the origins of Market Harborough are of the later 12th century, when it grew out of the village fields. In 1776, enclosures transformed the parish from four great medieval common fields to a pattern of straight fences and quick-grow planting, a process unwelcome to many; their feelings were well expressed by the Northamptonshire poet John Clare in his cri de coeur 'Enclosure', where he says:

Enclosure came, and trampled on the grave
Of labourers rights, and left the poor a slave:
And memories pride, ere want to wealth did bow.
In both the shadow and the substance now.

The Grand Union Canal was driven into the west of the village early in the 19th century, and some fifty years later the railway arrived to herald an industrial age.

Market Harborough, High Street 1922 72270
A deserted street funnels into the town centre: Sunday morning perhaps? Beyond the high brick wall with its iron restraints, a very good array of Georgian houses lead the eye into the market place and on to St Dionysius Church.

Market Harborough, St Nicholas Church, Little Bowden 1922 72276
Swallowed up by the suburbs of Market Harborough, this little village has managed to salvage some individuality. The small medieval church with its double bellcote form a centrepiece to a few houses of interest, including the Rectory of 1827 and the old Manor House of 1700.

Market Harborough, St Dionysius Church and the Old Grammar School 1922 72266
The classic market-town juxtaposition of church and grammar school create an ideal composition. The beautiful crocketted spire soars above the town, almost dwarfing the pretty timber-faced school building. In the background, behind the school, is the Symingtons Corset Factory.

Market Harborough, Leicester Road 1922 72271
This was a rural tree-lined road where children could feel at ease and little danger threatened to befall the solitary cyclist. Now, cars leaving the town centre accelerate up and away towards Gallows Hill and The Kibworths.

Market Harborough, The Old Grammar School c1955 M33021
In the 18th century, the almost picturesque group of church and school was completed by the addition of the town stocks and whipping post. The high quality timberwork in this essentially early 17th-century building is visible in the open ground floor. The exterior of the upper storey consists of modern boarding and pargeted plaster.

Market Harborough, High Street c1965 M33094
Just to the north of the church, the buildings on the west side of the road take on a varied appearance, the most specia being the Three Swans Hotel, which has its origins from at least the early 17th century. Boots the Chemist offers just a glimpse of 60s design, while Woolworths appear to have changed little since the 1930s.

CROCKATTS
THE TALBOT
TEAS
HOVIS
CAFE
INVICTA
BACON
XBD 762

Market Harborough, High Street c1965
M33039
Gone are the market stalls and booths of an earlier era. Here are the vans and accoutrements of a modern thriving market town, utilising the fronts of the Georgian buildings. The shops on the left of the photograph probably conceal timber frames of the 17th century or earlier.

◄ **Market Harborough, The Square c1955** M33012
A classic view of a market town. The open space around the square and the High Street to the north is bounded by well-mannered Georgian houses. 19th-century encroachments on the right do not distract from the beauty of the church, which dominates the photograph.

◄ **Market Harborough, The Memorial Cross 1922** 72265
Market Harborough's tribute to the fallen occupies pride of place in The Square, originally called the Sheep Market, which lies at the southern end of the market place. Behind the cross, Adam and Eve Street leads up to the former corsetry factory. Over the years encroachments have closed down this open space, but this may be excused by the quality of the flat-fronted Georgian buildings in the photograph.

▼ **Market Harborough, Foxton Locks c1965** M33107
From the foot of the Foxton flight of locks, the canal cuts through the classic late 18th-century enclosure landscape of straight hedges. The canal was built here in 1808-14, and a narrowboat trip through the ten locks would take about an hour. The cottage to the left and the elegant brick bridge would appear to be contemporary with the date of the canal. Because of the length of time it took to go through the locks, an inclined plane was built between 1897-1900, which raised or lowered the narrowboats from one end to the other in under ten minutes. By about 1930 this amazing piece of engineering was in a state of disuse and the metal parts were sold as scrap. The extant remains have been classed as an Ancient Monument, but at the time of writing they are in a slowly decaying condition and included in the Register of Buildings At Risk published by English Heritage.

◄ **Market Harborough, The Canal Bridge 1922** 72272
Designed and constructed as a working tool, canals have become some of the most attractive and restful waterways in Britain. The rawness of the original cut has softened, and bridges have about them a mellowness so apparent in this photograph.

Market Harborough, The Wooden Bridge 1922 72273
Just a plain wooden bridge, but it was a bridge such as this upon which Edward Thomas stood in 1915 when for a few moments he imagined himself to linger between the past and the future, or between life and death. He later expressed these feelings beautifully in his poem 'The Bridge'.

Market Harborough, Canal Boat Houses 1922 72274
The canal with its towing path, a symbol of an industrial age, has taken on a mantle of leisure. The bridge, contemporary with the cutting of the waterway, provides an ideal backdrop to the little armada of pleasure craft.

Market Harborough, Foxton Locks c1965 M33105
From the wide basin at the foot of the locks the prospect of climbing the flight by narrow boat is daunting. The area incorporating this once purely industrial facility, has now become a popular choice as an afternoon excursion into the country to escape from the city.

Great Bowden, The Green and the Village 1922 72275
This photograph shows this Domesday village, now much consumed by the tentacles of Market Harborough's suburbs, with its large irregular green and attractive houses, some dating back to 1567 and 1664, and Stone House in main Street to 1671. The stumpy spire of the mainly 15th-century church of St Peter and St Paul pokes above the rooftops, readily identifiable by its high lucarnes.

◄ **Kibworth Beauchamp, The Cricket Ground c1955** K119002

The cricket field is a focal point of village life, where summer upon summer old rivalries are played out. Here winter game plans hatched in the local pub can produce unlikely heroes, or fall apart in minutes. This is the battlefield - a small, probably balding, grass square.

Kibworth Beauchamp

The parish of Kibworth originally bracketed together Kibworth Beauchamp, Kibworth Harcourt and Smeeton Westerby; they shared the mother church of St Wilfred, which stands prominently on the north-south link road between the two Kibworths. Beauchamp was added to the original name through Walter de Beauchamp, Lord of the Manor c1130. It is a red-brick village with a few buildings of interest, such as the 17th-century Stuart House in Station Street and the Old Manor House in the High Street. Following the enclosure of the village around 1797, many agricultural workers were forced to find a new living in the hosiery industry.

◄ **Kibworth Beauchamp, The Square from the West c1960** K119019
George Lynn advertises his wares with considerable vigour on the south side of the triangular square, originally called Cross Bank. Nothing appears in the photograph to shake the post-war calm of the village, bypassed on its eastern side by the busy A6. The telephone box serves as a vivid reminder of so many that were destroyed, and replaced by ill-conceived 1990s substitutes.

◄ **Kibworth Harcourt, The Old Mill c1960**
K119033
Dated 1711, this last post-mill in the country ceased working in 1912. With its two pairs of stones, the design is such that the weatherboarded superstructure revolves round a central post, ensuring that the four great sails are always in the optimum position to take advantage of any available wind

▲

South Wigston, Crow Mill c1960 S548008

Crow Mill on the River Sence was recorded around the mid 12th century; we see it here in a picturesque meadowland setting. Close to the canal, it was bought by the canal's owners, and with the installation of a steam engine it worked until around 1900.

◄ **South Wigston, Blaby Road c1960** S548023

It was W G Hoskins who said of South Wigston that 'it reaches the rock bottom of English provincial life', and it would be hard to disagree with his sentiments. The railway, factories and the brick terraces are to be avoided unless travelling from the M1 to Oadby, or to the racecourse.

South Wigston & Wigston Magna

As late as 1870, enclosure meadowland and hawthorn hedges stretched away from Wigston Magna; but the ensuing period up to 1900 was to see a trebling in population figures, and the appearance of hosiers and boot and shoe manufacturers from Leicester, looking for potential factory sites. By 1885, thanks to the endeavours of Orson Wright, a speculative developer, the grid pattern of streets and terraces had begun to be laid down to house the influx of workers. Engine sheds bounded the railway, along with the new brick and tile works. Many people arrived to take up employment in this small booming new town, and in 1894 it became an Urban District, in a period of rolling industrialisation. Epitomising working life, a Mechanics' Institute, a National School, and a Working Men's Club were built for what amounted to a new style of society. Finally, public utilities were installed to complete what we now perceive as a picture of Victorian industry.

Four miles south of Leicester, medieval Wigston was a large nucleated village, standing in the middle of its three great fields. With the 1766 enclosure award came a replanned landscape of small fields overlying the former ridge and furrow furlongs, and industrialisation, which increased its population, brought with it fever and consumption to raise the death rate. Leicester's well-organised hosiery manufacturers hired out their knitting frames to smaller village masters, who, in turn, rented them to their operatives. The first railway station opened in 1839 and a second in 1957, with at one time some 300 railway workers living in Station Road. Victorian buildings began to blot out the earlier village street pattern, with the appearance of red-brick workers' cottages, a National School, and a Mechanics' Institute. A Framework Knitting Museum is open to the public in Bishloe End. Of Wigston's churches, All Saints dates from c1300, but St Whistans, although superficially medieval, was built in 1853. W G Hoskins' book, 'The Midland Peasant', written in 1957, paints a wonderful word-picture of the village from its origins to 1900.

Wigston Magna, The Memorial Park c1960
W366052
In the angle between Long Street and Chapel Lane lies this absolutely classic example of a municipal memorial park. The serpentine edging, designer boulders and statutory pavilion are to be seen in almost every suburb of Leicester in varied forms.

Hinckley, Castle Street c1965 H266006

The presence of ladies in hats, and of skirts below the knee, point unmistakably to a date in the mid-1960s, reinforced by the presence of a Silver Cross pram. A few late Georgian buildings brighten up this otherwise dull street-scene. At least the shops still retain well-mannered fronts.

Hinckley, Cosby & Lutterworth

Of ancient Hinchelie nothing remains. Of 12th-century Hinkelai the flattened castle mound has little to say, and the small Benedictine cell founded here in c1175 was disbanded prior to the Reformation. Of the parish church of The Assumption of St Mary, the 14th-century tower oversees much that is Victorian, with some work in 1877 by that rather uninspiring architect Ewan Christian.

It was in 1640 that the seeds of a successful industrial future were sown at Hinkley with the arrival of the home stocking-frame industry. Houses were rapidly adapted to accommodate the new machines, and prosperity reigned until setbacks in the early 1800s caused a total reversal of fortunes for the townsfolk. Although dominated by Leicester's hosiery industry, later 19th-century textile and boot and shoe factories were built in the town, bringing in their wake streets of red brick workers' houses. This is not really a place to saunter round for pleasure on a summer's evening.

Cosby is not enhanced by the presence of the M1 motorway on its eastern flank, or by the fact that the horny hand of industrial south Leicester has touched the village. Of its early history little remains, except a few hundred houses, and the Church of St Michael with its 15th-century tower and some earlier fabric. Quite rarely for Leicestershire, a cruck-framed barn survives in part at Church Farm close to the church.

During the 16th century, the village was dominated by the Bent family: firstly William and subsequently his son Thomas, who bought land here on a large scale, until by 1550 he owned well over 600 acres within the parish. By contrast, in 1615 the vicar of Cosby was complaining bitterly that he could not support his family on a wage of under five pounds a year.

Little more than a village before the 18th century, Lutterworth is famous for its association with John Wycliff, a religious reformer and translator of the bible, who was condemned by the Pope in 1377 for his outspoken attacks on clerical wealth and privilege. Wycliffe came to Lutterworth in the wake of this condemnation as rector, under the protection of John of Gaunt, where he was to die in 1384. He did not rest in peace: his remains were exhumed and burnt in 1428, and the remnants thrown into the River Swift. The church, which is not without interest, has a good white marble monument to Wycliffe in the south aisle, by Richard Westmacott and dated 1837.

The town, with its town hall designed in 1836 by Joseph Aloysius Hansom, inventor of the hansom cab, comprises buildings mainly of the earlier 19th century, but notwithstanding this, the High Street, Market Place and Market Street are worthy of inspection. In 1218 the Hospital of St John The Baptist was established at Lutterworth for the poor and aged, but it was dissolved and lost about 1580.

▼ Hinckley, Castle Street c1965 H266010

A collection of almost classic cars parked on both sides of the street issues a warning of things to come in the small towns around Leicestershire. In a street of mainly late 19th- and early 20th-century buildings, the uncomfortable all-purpose shop fronts of the 1960s on the left warn of an equal disaster in the world of architecture. Note the original shop fronts in the building to the right of the photograph.

▼ Cosby, The Brook c1965 C433007

The brook here somehow appears to be little cared for, with its chipped concrete posts arrayed along weedy banks. To the right of the photograph is a row of uninteresting 19th/20th-century houses; to the left, and of an earlier era, is a three-story, three-bay brick farmhouse, so common in Leicestershire villages. The overall scene is not enhanced by telephone wires and a rather nasty bus shelter.

▲ Cosby, Main Street c1965 C433008

The openness of the village is readily apparent in this photograph: it ranges along a brook, criss-crossed by modest Urban District Council railed footbridges. Regrettably, the main 19th-century two-storey buildings fail to enhance the scene to a degree that can be called picturesque.

◄ **Lutterworth, The Denbigh Arms, High Street c1955** L307001

This is a typical atmospheric Georgian hotel on the steep hill up through the town. Although the front of the building is of early 19th-century appearance, earlier brickwork and, indeed, some signs of timber framing within the buildings speak of a longer history.

CHEMIST
Ucal
PURE
ICES

Lutterworth, Church Street c1955 L307005
Church Street has about it an almost faded Dickensian air, in tune with a town whose better days appear to be past, which is a great pity. The photograph shows congenial, modest, mostly early 19th-century buildings, with a series of shop fronts pre-dating the ugliness of late 20th-century aluminium framing and internally illuminated fascia signs.

▲
Market Bosworth, The Town c1955 M233001
Since the 13th century there has been a market here, and the buildings in the town centre reflect a gentle change rather than a dramatic fluctuation of fortune at any one time. Single-storey dormered cottages sit comfortably with the later elegance of the flat-fronted Georgian house further along the street.

Market Bosworth

The Dixies brought a certain amount of prosperity to the town when they built the hall at the end of the 17th century in the shadow of the church, which at the end of the previous century was itself providing a particularly rich living. From the red-brick house it is a rewarding saunter through the park to Sutton Cheney church, and to the Battlefield Centre at Ambion Hill Farm. The battle, fought on 22 August 1485, is easily visualised through illustrative boards set discreetly round the site. An easy walk back to the town completes a circle of about five miles, but tea and cakes are not easily come by to round off the walk.

Fortunately, the town totally escaped the destructive influences that assailed its close neighbours in the coalfields, such as Desford and Nailstone. Fox coverts spread around the town are a reminder that Leicestershire provides ideal hunting country, but for the lovers of speed the motor race track at Kirby Mallory provides more than adequate entertainment.

Market Bosworth, The Church c1960 M233025

Market Bosworth, The Market Square c1955 M233015
Market Bosworth was granted the privilege of a Wednesday market in 1285, and the small town was one of 29 in the country to combine this with an annual fair. In a primarily subsistence-orientated world, the market of the 13th century proved an efficient way for producers to sell their surplus products. More often than not the privilege of establishing a market had to be bought, and the lord needed to be sure of a return on his investment. The Market Square, which here takes a triangular form, is surrounded by modest, attractive, mainly 18th-century houses, apart from the Grammar School, which, to some extent, raises the scale. The presence of a traditional but modern cross completes the picture. Today the square has regrettably taken on a more regimented appearance, with a regularised car park behind concrete bollards, but it is, in its essentials, little changed. Situated away from major routes, the town has derived its fame from the Battle of 1485, when Henry Tudor, later Henry VII, defeated Richard III on Ambion Hill to its south.

A444

Twycross

Twycross is not surrounded by villages of outstanding interest, but to its east is Gopsall Park, on the site of Gopsall, the deserted medieval village. The house, built by Charles Jennens in 1747, and designed by John Westley, a local architect, in a loosely Palladian manner, was the grandest house in West Leicestershire. In what amounts to an appalling act of vandalism the house was demolished in 1951. The village is not well equipped with vernacular houses of special quality, but the Old Hall near the church must be noted.

Although mainly of the early 14th century, the architecture of the church takes a very definite second place to the magnificent medieval east window. Said to have come from the Saint-Chapelle in Paris and presented to King William IV, it is a breath-taking example of the 13th-century French stained-glass artists' work. Many visitors come to Twycross for the zoo, but stop off in the village to see a superb work of art.

Twycross, The Village Street c1960 T237006
Its position on the A444 between Nuneaton and Burton-on-Trent is belied in this rural idyll. The cows with their driver, the cottages ranged behind small gardens and picket fences, and the church tower in the background, add up to a satisfactory whole, of which William Morris would have approved.

◄ **Ashby-de-la-Zouch, The Castle c1965** A212029
Situated in the shadow of the grand church of St Helen's, the castle, now in the care of English Heritage, originated as a Norman manor house; it ultimately become the property of the Breton La Zouch family in the mid 12th century. Probably the castle's most famous, or infamous, owner was William Lord Hastings, who was beheaded by King Richard III in 1483.

Ashby-de-la-Zouch & Ibstock

If it had been sited a little further to the northwest, the market town of Ashby-de-la-Zouch would have been in Derbyshire. In the past this quiet town, which lies close to the remnants of the Leicestershire coalfields, was generally better known than it is today; it found an everlasting monument in the sweeping novels of Sir Walter Scott and in its spa, which opened around 1822 with the erection of the rather beautiful, but now demolished, Ivanhoe Baths and the Royal Hotel.

The origin of the name Ibstock is 'the Stoc of Ibba', a usage often allied to a monastic place, but here to a personal name. The settlement grew up in the Leicestershire coalfields along with its close neighbours Coalville, Nailstone, Bagworth and Ellistown. The discovery of suitable clay for brick making in 1830 led to the opening of a second industry, which continues today.

◄ **Ashby-de-la-Zouch, Old Cottages, Hill Street c1955** A212014
Here we see pretty brick and stone cottages of the 18th century and earlier, which went to make up the Ashby referred to by Camden as 'villa amoenissima'; they pre-date the dramatic launch of the town as a health-restoring spa.

◄ **Ashby-de-la-Zouch, The Royal Hotel, Station Road c1965**
A212033
The Royal Hotel is an impressive brick and stone building, designed by the virtually unknown architect Robert Chaplin in 1826; he employed a large porch of paired Greek Doric columns to impress those arriving in search of the invigorating spa waters, which were said to be good for rheumatism.

◄ **Ashby-de-la-Zouch, View from St Helen's Church c1965** A212030

This view looks from St Helen's Church, west across the rooftops, to Our Lady of Lourdes RC Church and Holy Trinity Church in Kilwardby Street. The countrywide low point of early 1960s building design has clearly arrived at Ashby, with the larger building towards the bottom right of the photograph standing out in an otherwise well-ordered townscape.

◄ **Ashby-de-la-Zouch, Market Street c1955**
A212012
The slightly overlarge Italianate Town Hall, along with the French Renaissance bank building of 1891, dominate an otherwise well-ordered street scene. The buildings appear to be of later Georgian date, but the jettied timber-framed house to the right speaks of hidden treasures to be found behind and within.

▼ **Ashby-de-la-Zouch, Market Street c1965**
A212017
This pleasant but rather undistinguished wide street was the scene of a Saturday market since it was granted in 1219. The photograph generally shows later Georgian flat-fronted houses with shops thrust into their ground floors.

▲ **Ibstock, St Denys' Church c1965** I48003
Archbishop Laud was at some time rector of this rather fine church, which forms a pleasant group with the 18th-century vicarage at the southern end of this mining town. Although it is almost entirely of the 14th century, it has few interior features to detain the visitor.

Coalville, Belvoir Road c1956 C4323126
This photograph shows perhaps one of the less depressing views that can be taken in the town, but even in 1956, the pattern of things to come is readily apparent in the intrusive shopfront and canopy pushed into a reasonably attractive facade.

Coalville
& Mount St Bernard Abbey

It is not possible to think of Coalville without thinking of Desford, Whitwick, Ellistown and Merry Lees, all pits in the Leicestershire coalfields which provided generations of miners with a dangerous, unforgiving living, until the end arrived with the closure of Bagworth Colliery in 1991.

For some five hundred years the area has been mined, but in 1824 deep mining arrived at Whitwick, and by 1833 the aptly named Coalville had been born. The town grew with the expansion of the industry, and with the arrival of the railway which opened in 1833, to blend inexorably with the surrounding unloveliness of the pit-heads and tips. Much of the evidence of coal mining has now disappeared, but at Snibstone, to the north-west of the town, a sanitised glimpse of mining life can be had at the Discovery Park.

Situated on the edge of the Charnwood Forest, some two miles from Whitwick, Mount St Bernard Abbey, which was founded here in 1835, was the first Cistercian house in England since the dissolution of the monasteries. The buildings occupy land given to the monastery in 1835 by Ambrose Lisle March-Phillips of Grace Dieu Manor and sponsored by the Earl of Shrewsbury. Much of the building work was done by the community.

◄ **Coalville, Jackson Street c1965** C432045
Small, well-mannered cottages set a later 19th-century scene in the days before parked cars lined the roads. The bay-windowed house to the left of the photograph remains intact but neglected, while shops have taken over the remainder.

◄ **Coalville, Leicester Road c1965** C432053
A depressing series of small-scale shops line the main road, which is soon to sweep in more peaceful mode under Bardon Hill. Few of the shop fronts are of any quality: in particular, 'Telefusion' serves to herald the dawn of the visually unattractive 1960s.

▼ **Coalville, Roundabout c1965** C432007
Almost out of shot on the right-hand side of the photograph is probably the best-quality structure in the town. Designed by Henry Collings in 1926 and faced in brick and stone, the Clock Tower overshadows Memorial Square and the market place.

◄ **Coalville, The Shopping Centre c1965** C432054
This could be any town, anywhere, the epitome of the Borough Architects' brave new world of the early 1960s. More shopper-friendly enclosed arcades have taken the place of the violently unattractive centres, and no-one can mourn their passing.

Mount St Bernard Abbey, From the East c1965 C432034
The church to the left of the photograph remained incomplete until just prior to the outset of World War II; construction work had stopped in 1844 through a lack of finances. The well-proportioned tower, which sits above the sanctuary, was designed by the Leicester architect Albert Herbert and completed in 1939.

◄ **Mount St Bernard Abbey, From the North-West c1965**
C432035
This monastic group faced in local granite rubble with ashlar dressings was carefully designed by A W N Pugin to meet the relatively austere needs of a Cistercian house. Completed in 1841, the Guest House with its central carriage opening occupies much of the photograph. To the left of the shot are the lancet lights to the Monastic Choir of 1843-4.

Mount St Bernard Abbey, The Clock Tower c1965 ► C4323001
The clock tower with its slated spire-like roof sits on the western range of the claustral buildings, above the enclosed garden to its west and the small cloister to its east. The tower was added in 1871.

◄ **Mount St Bernard Abbey, The Calvary c1965** C4323004
This dramatic view of the Calvary, which lies to the north of the Abbey buildings, was taken shortly after its completion, with the addition of the figure of Christ in 1965, although it was begun in 1847.

Castle Donington & Kegworth

The village, with its market place and church, grew up around the castle in much the same way as Totnes in Devon or Warkworth in Northumberland. The grid pattern of streets provide a vital clue to its medieval origins. Of the castle buildings nothing survives; in fact, the site is now given over to houses and gardens. The castle was eventually forsaken for the more amenable pleasure of the hall and park, but it was not until the parish enclosure of 1777 that the tightly-packed villagers moved out into more airy accommodation in the surrounding fields, many of which are now obliterated by the noisy East Midlands Airport.

Kegworth is now a rather benighted industrial village on the River Soar, but its origins lay in its medieval weekly market and annual fairs. The arrival of framework knitters heralded its transformation, culminating in a dour expansion in the form of redbrick housing and hosiery factories. Old houses of some merit are to be found in London Road, around the High Street and on Packington Hill. The grand church of St Andrew, although internally quite dull, justifies a visit.

Castle Donington, High Street c1955 C430001
Bondgate crosses Mount Pleasant to become the restrained High Street on the south side of the village rising up to Hill Top. The photographer looks back down the hill past 19th-century houses towards the village centre.

Castle Donington, The Church of St Edward King and Martyr c1955 C430014
Seen here from the south, the parish church with its unusual dedication is an amalgam of parts up to the 15th century, when the porch was added on the south side. Apart from the east window by Kemp and Co and a few minor monuments, there is little here to interest the visitor.

Castle Donington, The Key House, High Street c1955 C430003
Dating from the turn of the 17th century, the Key House is probably the best of Castle Donington's vernacular buildings. Timber-framed, it has a two-story porch decorated with lozenges, a most unusual feature for its date.

Castle Donington, Market Street c1955 C430005
The photograph is dominated by a brick and stone building typical of its turn-of-the-century date, but in this southern sector of the town earlier houses are to be found, including a stone-faced building in Apiary Gate of c1670.

Castle Donington, Kings Mill c1955
C430009

◄ **Castle Donington, Cottages at Kings Mills c1955** C430007

This terrace of almost picturesque millworkers' cottages now sits quietly, adjacent to the isolated and decaying great water wheels which once powered the mills. Originally for corn milling, the mills in their later life were given over to a variety of industrial uses.

▼ **Castle Donington, The River Trent at Kings Mills c1955** C430008

This is a leisurely view typical of many to be seen on the rivers Trent and Soar. The need to protect the crossing of this river provided the initial raison d'etre for the castle and the village.

◄ **Castle Donington, Bondgate c1955** C430004

Although quiet, even in 1955, Bondgate is on the line of the turnpike road between Long Easton and Ashby-de-la-Zouch. We can still appreciate in these photographs the quality of houses and shops, before the destructive work of the modern window salesman spread like a rash over the country.

Kegworth, View from St Andrews Church c1965 K139034
A view which highlights the growth of industrial Kegworth. In 1965 uncomfortably large utilitarian factory/stores nestle close to the church, among the irregular tiled roofs of an earlier era.

Kegworth, The Lock c1965 K139008
To the east of the village, we see a timeless view of an industry wiped out by the growth of the national railway system. Once utilised to deliver raw materials and to take away the finished products to Derby or to Leicester, the waterway is basically reduced to the status of a leisure facility.

Index

Frith Book Co Titles

www.francisfrith.co.uk

The Frith Book Company publishes over 100 new titles each year. A selection of those currently available are listed below. For latest catalogue please contact Frith Book Co.

Town Books 96 pages, approx 100 photos. County and Themed Books 128 pages, approx 150 photos (unless specified). All titles hardback laminated case and jacket except those indicated pb (paperback)

Amersham, Chesham & Rickmansworth (pb)	1-85937-340-2	£9.99
Ancient Monuments & Stone Circles	1-85937-143-4	£17.99
Aylesbury (pb)	1-85937-227-9	£9.99
Bakewell	1-85937-113-2	£12.99
Barnstaple (pb)	1-85937-300-3	£9.99
Bath (pb)	1-85937419-0	£9.99
Bedford (pb)	1-85937-205-8	£9.99
Berkshire (pb)	1-85937-191-4	£9.99
Berkshire Churches	1-85937-170-1	£17.99
Blackpool (pb)	1-85937-382-8	£9.99
Bognor Regis (pb)	1-85937-431-x	£9.99
Bournemouth	1-85937-067-5	£12.99
Bradford (pb)	1-85937-204-x	£9.99
Brighton & Hove(pb)	1-85937-192-2	£8.99
Bristol (pb)	1-85937-264-3	£9.99
British Life A Century Ago (pb)	1-85937-213-9	£9.99
Buckinghamshire (pb)	1-85937-200-7	£9.99
Camberley (pb)	1-85937-222-8	£9.99
Cambridge (pb)	1-85937-422-0	£9.99
Cambridgeshire (pb)	1-85937-420-4	£9.99
Canals & Waterways (pb)	1-85937-291-0	£9.99
Canterbury Cathedral (pb)	1-85937-179-5	£9.99
Cardiff (pb)	1-85937-093-4	£9.99
Carmarthenshire	1-85937-216-3	£14.99
Chelmsford (pb)	1-85937-310-0	£9.99
Cheltenham (pb)	1-85937-095-0	£9.99
Cheshire (pb)	1-85937-271-6	£9.99
Chester	1-85937-090-x	£12.99
Chesterfield	1-85937-378-x	£9.99
Chichester (pb)	1-85937-228-7	£9.99
Colchester (pb)	1-85937-188-4	£8.99
Cornish Coast	1-85937-163-9	£14.99
Cornwall (pb)	1-85937-229-5	£9.99
Cornwall Living Memories	1-85937-248-1	£14.99
Cotswolds (pb)	1-85937-230-9	£9.99
Cotswolds Living Memories	1-85937-255-4	£14.99
County Durham	1-85937-123-x	£14.99
Croydon Living Memories	1-85937-162-0	£9.99
Cumbria	1-85937-101-9	£14.99
Dartmoor	1-85937-145-0	£14.99
Derby (pb)	1-85937-367-4	£9.99
Derbyshire (pb)	1-85937-196-5	£9.99
Devon (pb)	1-85937-297-x	£9.99
Dorset (pb)	1-85937-269-4	£9.99
Dorset Churches	1-85937-172-8	£17.99
Dorset Coast (pb)	1-85937-299-6	£9.99
Dorset Living Memories	1-85937-210-4	£14.99
Down the Severn	1-85937-118-3	£14.99
Down the Thames (pb)	1-85937-278-3	£9.99
Down the Trent	1-85937-311-9	£14.99
Dublin (pb)	1-85937-231-7	£9.99
East Anglia (pb)	1-85937-265-1	£9.99
East London	1-85937-080-2	£14.99
East Sussex	1-85937-130-2	£14.99
Eastbourne	1-85937-061-6	£12.99
Edinburgh (pb)	1-85937-193-0	£8.99
England in the 1880s	1-85937-331-3	£17.99
English Castles (pb)	1-85937-434-4	£9.99
English Country Houses	1-85937-161-2	£17.99
Essex (pb)	1-85937-270-8	£9.99
Exeter	1-85937-126-4	£12.99
Exmoor	1-85937-132-9	£14.99
Falmouth	1-85937-066-7	£12.99
Folkestone (pb)	1-85937-124-8	£9.99
Glasgow (pb)	1-85937-190-6	£9.99
Gloucestershire	1-85937-102-7	£14.99
Great Yarmouth (pb)	1-85937-426-3	£9.99
Greater Manchester (pb)	1-85937-266-x	£9.99
Guildford (pb)	1-85937-410-7	£9.99
Hampshire (pb)	1-85937-279-1	£9.99
Hampshire Churches (pb)	1-85937-207-4	£9.99
Harrogate	1-85937-423-9	£9.99
Hastings & Bexhill (pb)	1-85937-131-0	£9.99
Heart of Lancashire (pb)	1-85937-197-3	£9.99
Helston (pb)	1-85937-214-7	£9.99
Hereford (pb)	1-85937-175-2	£9.99
Herefordshire	1-85937-174-4	£14.99
Hertfordshire (pb)	1-85937-247-3	£9.99
Horsham (pb)	1-85937-432-8	£9.99
Humberside	1-85937-215-5	£14.99
Hythe, Romney Marsh & Ashford	1-85937-256-2	£9.99

Available from your local bookshop or from the publisher

Frith Book Co Titles (continued)

Ipswich (pb)	1-85937-424-7	£9.99
Ireland (pb)	1-85937-181-7	£9.99
Isle of Man (pb)	1-85937-268-6	£9.99
Isles of Scilly	1-85937-136-1	£14.99
Isle of Wight (pb)	1-85937-429-8	£9.99
Isle of Wight Living Memories	1-85937-304-6	£14.99
Kent (pb)	1-85937-189-2	£9.99
Kent Living Memories	1-85937-125-6	£14.99
Lake District (pb)	1-85937-275-9	£9.99
Lancaster, Morecambe & Heysham (pb)	1-85937-233-3	£9.99
Leeds (pb)	1-85937-202-3	£9.99
Leicester	1-85937-073-x	£12.99
Leicestershire (pb)	1-85937-185-x	£9.99
Lincolnshire (pb)	1-85937-433-6	£9.99
Liverpool & Merseyside (pb)	1-85937-234-1	£9.99
London (pb)	1-85937-183-3	£9.99
Ludlow (pb)	1-85937-176-0	£9.99
Luton (pb)	1-85937-235-x	£9.99
Maidstone	1-85937-056-x	£14.99
Manchester (pb)	1-85937-198-1	£9.99
Middlesex	1-85937-158-2	£14.99
New Forest	1-85937-128-0	£14.99
Newark (pb)	1-85937-366-6	£9.99
Newport, Wales (pb)	1-85937-258-9	£9.99
Newquay (pb)	1-85937-421-2	£9.99
Norfolk (pb)	1-85937-195-7	£9.99
Norfolk Living Memories	1-85937-217-1	£14.99
Northamptonshire	1-85937-150-7	£14.99
Northumberland Tyne & Wear (pb)	1-85937-281-3	£9.99
North Devon Coast	1-85937-146-9	£14.99
North Devon Living Memories	1-85937-261-9	£14.99
North London	1-85937-206-6	£14.99
North Wales (pb)	1-85937-298-8	£9.99
North Yorkshire (pb)	1-85937-236-8	£9.99
Norwich (pb)	1-85937-194-9	£8.99
Nottingham (pb)	1-85937-324-0	£9.99
Nottinghamshire (pb)	1-85937-187-6	£9.99
Oxford (pb)	1-85937-411-5	£9.99
Oxfordshire (pb)	1-85937-430-1	£9.99
Peak District (pb)	1-85937-280-5	£9.99
Penzance	1-85937-069-1	£12.99
Peterborough (pb)	1-85937-219-8	£9.99
Piers	1-85937-237-6	£17.99
Plymouth	1-85937-119-1	£12.99
Poole & Sandbanks (pb)	1-85937-251-1	£9.99
Preston (pb)	1-85937-212-0	£9.99
Reading (pb)	1-85937-238-4	£9.99
Romford (pb)	1-85937-319-4	£9.99
Salisbury (pb)	1-85937-239-2	£9.99
Scarborough (pb)	1-85937-379-8	£9.99
St Albans (pb)	1-85937-341-0	£9.99
St Ives (pb)	1-85937415-8	£9.99
Scotland (pb)	1-85937-182-5	£9.99
Scottish Castles (pb)	1-85937-323-2	£9.99
Sevenoaks & Tunbridge	1-85937-057-8	£12.99
Sheffield, South Yorks (pb)	1-85937-267-8	£9.99
Shrewsbury (pb)	1-85937-325-9	£9.99
Shropshire (pb)	1-85937-326-7	£9.99
Somerset	1-85937-153-1	£14.99
South Devon Coast	1-85937-107-8	£14.99
South Devon Living Memories	1-85937-168-x	£14.99
South Hams	1-85937-220-1	£14.99
Southampton (pb)	1-85937-427-1	£9.99
Southport (pb)	1-85937-425-5	£9.99
Staffordshire	1-85937-047-0	£12.99
Stratford upon Avon	1-85937-098-5	£12.99
Suffolk (pb)	1-85937-221-x	£9.99
Suffolk Coast	1-85937-259-7	£14.99
Surrey (pb)	1-85937-240-6	£9.99
Sussex (pb)	1-85937-184-1	£9.99
Swansea (pb)	1-85937-167-1	£9.99
Tees Valley & Cleveland	1-85937-211-2	£14.99
Thanet (pb)	1-85937-116-7	£9.99
Tiverton (pb)	1-85937-178-7	£9.99
Torbay	1-85937-063-2	£12.99
Truro	1-85937-147-7	£12.99
Victorian and Edwardian Cornwall	1-85937-252-x	£14.99
Victorian & Edwardian Devon	1-85937-253-8	£14.99
Victorian & Edwardian Kent	1-85937-149-3	£14.99
Vic & Ed Maritime Album	1-85937-144-2	£17.99
Victorian and Edwardian Sussex	1-85937-157-4	£14.99
Victorian & Edwardian Yorkshire	1-85937-154-x	£14.99
Victorian Seaside	1-85937-159-0	£17.99
Villages of Devon (pb)	1-85937-293-7	£9.99
Villages of Kent (pb)	1-85937-294-5	£9.99
Villages of Sussex (pb)	1-85937-295-3	£9.99
Warwickshire (pb)	1-85937-203-1	£9.99
Welsh Castles (pb)	1-85937-322-4	£9.99
West Midlands (pb)	1-85937-289-9	£9.99
West Sussex	1-85937-148-5	£14.99
West Yorkshire (pb)	1-85937-201-5	£9.99
Weymouth (pb)	1-85937-209-0	£9.99
Wiltshire (pb)	1-85937-277-5	£9.99
Wiltshire Churches (pb)	1-85937-171-x	£9.99
Wiltshire Living Memories	1-85937-245-7	£14.99
Winchester (pb)	1-85937-428-x	£9.99
Windmills & Watermills	1-85937-242-2	£17.99
Worcester (pb)	1-85937-165-5	£9.99
Worcestershire	1-85937-152-3	£14.99
York (pb)	1-85937-199-x	£9.99
Yorkshire (pb)	1-85937-186-8	£9.99
Yorkshire Living Memories	1-85937-166-3	£14.99

Frith Products & Services

Francis Frith would doubtless be pleased to know that the pioneering publishing venture he started in 1860 still continues today. A hundred and forty years later, The Francis Frith Collection continues in the same innovative tradition and is now one of the foremost publishers of vintage photographs in the world. Some of the current activities include:

Interior Decoration

Today Frith's photographs can be seen framed and as giant wall murals in thousands of pubs, restaurants, hotels, banks, retail stores and other public buildings throughout the country. In every case they enhance the unique local atmosphere of the places they depict and provide reminders of gentler days in an increasingly busy and frenetic world.

Product Promotions

Frith products are used by many major companies to promote the sales of their own products or to reinforce their own history and heritage. Frith promotions have been used by Hovis bread, Courage beers, Scots Porage Oats, Colman's mustard, Cadbury's foods, Mellow Birds coffee, Dunhill pipe tobacco, Guinness, and Bulmer's Cider.

Genealogy and Family History

As the interest in family history and roots grows world-wide, more and more people are turning to Frith's photographs of Great Britain for images of the towns, villages and streets where their ancestors lived; and, of course, photographs of the churches and chapels where their ancestors were christened, married and buried are an essential part of every genealogy tree and family album.

Frith Products

All Frith photographs are available Framed or just as Mounted Prints and Posters (size 23 x 16 inches). These may be ordered from the address below. From time to time other products - Address Books, Calendars, Table Mats, etc - are available.

The Internet

Already twenty thousand Frith photographs can be viewed and purchased on the internet through the Frith websites and a myriad of partner sites.

For more detailed information on Frith companies and products, look at these sites:

www.francisfrith.co.uk
www.francisfrith.com
(for North American visitors)

See the complete list of Frith Books at:
www.francisfrith.co.uk

This web site is regularly updated with the latest list of publications from the Frith Book Company. If you wish to buy books relating to another part of the country that your local bookshop does not stock, you may purchase on-line.

For further information, trade, or author enquiries please contact us at the address below:

The Francis Frith Collection, Frith's Barn, Teffont, Salisbury, Wiltshire, England SP3 5QP.
Tel: +44 (0)1722 716 376 Fax: +44 (0)1722 716 881 Email: sales@francisfrith.co.uk

See Frith books on the internet www.francisfrith.co.uk

To receive your FREE Mounted Print

Mounted Print
Overall size 14 x 11 inches

Cut out this Voucher and return it with your remittance for £1.95 to cover postage and handling, to UK addresses. For overseas addresses please include £4.00 post and handling. Choose any photograph included in this book. Your SEPIA print will be A4 in size, and mounted in a cream mount with burgundy rule line, overall size 14 x 11inches.

Order additional Mounted Prints at HALF PRICE (only £7.49 each*)
If there are further pictures you would like to order, possibly as gifts for friends and family, purchase them at half price (no additional postage and handling required).

Have your Mounted Prints framed*
For an additional £14.95 per print you can have your chosen Mounted Print framed in an elegant polished wood and gilt moulding, overall size 16 x 13 inches (no additional postage and handling required).

*** IMPORTANT!**
These special prices are only available if ordered using the original voucher on this page (no copies permitted) and at the same time as your free Mounted Print, for delivery to the same address

Frith Collectors' Guild

From time to time we publish a magazine of news and stories about Frith photographs and further special offers of Frith products. If you would like 12 months FREE membership, please return this form.

Send completed forms to:
The Francis Frith Collection, Frith's Barn, Teffont, Salisbury, Wiltshire SP3 5QP

Voucher for FREE and Reduced Price Frith Prints

Picture no.	Page number	Qty	Mounted @ £7.49	Framed + £14.95	Total Cost
		1	**Free of charge***	£	£
			£7.49	£	£
			£7.49	£	£
			£7.49	£	£
			£7.49	£	£
			£7.49	£	£

Please allow 28 days for delivery — *** Post & handling** — **£1.95**

Book Title . . . . **Total Order Cost** **£**

Please do not photocopy this voucher. Only the original is valid, so please cut it out and return it to us.

I enclose a cheque / postal order for £ . . . .
made payable to 'The Francis Frith Collection'
OR please debit my Mastercard / Visa / Switch / Amex card
(credit cards please on all overseas orders)

Number . . . .

Issue No (Switch only) . . . . Valid from (Amex/Switch) . . . .

Expires . . . . Signature . . . .

Name Mr/Mrs/Ms ....

Address ....

....

....

.... Postcode ....

Daytime Tel No ....

Valid to 31/12/03

The Francis Frith Collectors' Guild

Please enrol me as a member for 12 months free of charge.

Name Mr/Mrs/Ms ....

Address ....

....

....

.... Postcode ....

Free Print - see overleaf

Would you like to find out more about Francis Frith?

We have recently recruited some entertaining speakers who are happy to visit local groups, clubs and societies to give an illustrated talk documenting Frith's travels and photographs. If you are a member of such a group and are interested in hosting a presentation, we would love to hear from you.

Our speakers bring with them a small selection of our local town and county books, together with sample prints. They are happy to take orders. A small proportion of the order value is donated to the group who have hosted the presentation. The talks are therefore an excellent way of fundraising for small groups and societies.

Can you help us with information about any of the Frith photographs in this book?

We are gradually compiling an historical record for each of the photographs in the Frith archive. It is always fascinating to find out the names of the people shown in the pictures, as well as insights into the shops, buildings and other features depicted.

If you recognize anyone in the photographs in this book, or if you have information not already included in the author's caption, do let us know. We would love to hear from you, and will try to publish it in future books or articles.

Our production team

Frith books are produced by a small dedicated team at offices in the converted Grade II listed 18th-century barn at Teffont near Salisbury, illustrated above. Most have worked with the Frith Collection for many years. All have in common one quality: they have a passion for the Frith Collection. The team is constantly expanding, but currently includes:

Jason Buck, John Buck, Douglas Burns, Heather Crisp, Lucy Elcock, Isobel Hall, Rob Hames, Hazel Heaton, Peter Horne, James Kinnear, Tina Leary, Hannah Marsh, Eliza Sackett, Terence Sackett, Sandra Sanger, Lewis Taylor, Shelley Tolcher, Helen Vimpany, Clive Wathen and Jenny Wathen.